JESSICA TYNER

AN IMPRINT OF

TAYEN LANE

PUBLISHING

COPYRIGHT

Copyright © 2014 by Jessica Tyner

All rights reserved.

ISBN (Hardcover) 978-0-9906614-1-2

In accordance with the U.S. Copyright Act of 1976, the scanning, uploading, and electronic sharing of any part of this book without permission of the publisher constitute unlawful piracy and theft of the author's intellectual property. No part of this book may be reproduced or transmitted in any form or by any means, electronic or mechanical, including photocopying, recording, or by any information storage and retrieval system, except for excerpts used for reviews, without permission in writing from the publisher.

Edited by Bri Bruce

Cover painting courtesy Catherine Chauloux

Cover design Tayen Lane Publishing

ACKNOWLEDGEMENTS

Without Chintan Mehta, few of these poems would have been written and this book wouldn't exist. You are my great love, my partner, my muse. Love you more.

Thank you to my mom, Rita Tyner, who always believed in me, and my late father, Johnnie Tyner. I've done my best to capture his spirit in these pages, though that can never fully be achieved.

Finally, an enormous thank you to Tayen Lane Publishing who took a chance on my work and me. Thank you for your support, guidance, and all the hard work from incredible editors who are skilled and talented beyond belief. You've done magic with my words.

DEDICATION

For Chintan (of course).

TABLE OF CONTENTS

PART ONE   2
    CHILDHOOD & FAMILY

CHILDHOOD   4

BUTTERFLY STORMS   6

THE SACRAMENT   8

END OF THE HARVEST SEASON   10

FOR MY FATHER   12

PASSING   14

TO THE BONE   16

THE MEATWORKS   18

TWO DAYS PRIOR TO THE BURIAL   20

PART TWO   22
    COSTA RICA

SPELEOLOGY   24

EN MORAVIA   26

THE CARVING STATION   28

PINKY SWEARS AND KITCHEN CHAIRS   30

HOLY WEEK AT PLAYA NEGRA   32

LOVE YOU MORE   34

INSIDE THE ROSEMARY BUSH   36

LEAVE TWO POUNDS OF SKIN   38

THE ROAD PAST CARTAGO   40

THE CATAMARAN   42

THE BANANA PLANTATION   44

PART THREE 46
 THE MIDDLE EAST

CALL TO PRAYER 48

I THOUGHT YOU WERE PRAYING 50

RACING CAMELS 52

SOMETHING SWEET 54

PART FOUR 56
 THE SELF

SAVAGERY 58

OUTSIDE THE BOXING GYM 60

HOW I LIKE MY WOMEN 62

THE LECTURE 64

BOUQUET OF THE BODY 66

GENETICALLY ISOLATED SINCE THE ICE AGE 68

ON THE RUNWAY 70

BATTLE SCARS 72

"EATING LIKE A BIRD, IT'S REALLY A FALSITY" —NORMAN BATES 74

PART FIVE 76
 LOVE (THE EARLY YEARS)

CHOREOGRAPHY 78

HOW TO OIL AN INDIAN MAN'S HAIR 80

THE 82

THINGS MAHAVIRA DOESN'T KNOW 84

CHRISTMAS CHAI 86

ANATOMY OF A TRUNK 88

EATING 90

LIMITS OF THE TONGUE   92

DRAG ME THROUGH THE MESS   94

THE LAST EXOTIC PETTING ZOO   96

RECIPE FOR MOONG DAAL   98

THE PHOTOGRAPH   100

SYMPTOMS OF AN END   102

NIGHT BEFORE MUMBAI   104

PART SIX   106
    LOVE (THE FALLOUT)

BRONCO BUSTING   108

FOR THE ANIMALS   110

A WEDNESDAY AFTERNOON   112

VALENTINE'S DAY   114

FILTHY TIGER CHAI SOAP   116

THE SALT LICK   118

INSIDE THE DEVIL'S PUNCH BOWL   120

HOW DYING IS DONE   122

OF TRANS AMS AND CHICKENS   124

WHAT I FOUND IN THE SWAMP   126

PART SEVEN   128
    LOVE (RESURRECTION)

ASHIATSU IN THE BEDROOM   130

ON BEAUTY AND LOVE   132

PRODUCE   134

'FLORA' AND 'FAWNA'   136

KITCHEN VOLCANOES   138

THE SWEET BELOW THE BITTER   140

BEAUTIFUL   142

PART EIGHT   144
   LOVE (MUMBAI)

FAMILIAL TERRITORY   146

DO YOU SEE THE STARS?   148

LURE   150

PART NINE   152
   LOVE

SATYAVACHAN   154

THE THINGS I DO FOR YOU   156

SAVING ROOM   158

THE PROPOSAL   160

36 HOURS   162

RESURRECTION   164

ALL THE UNSAID THINGS   166

THE PROTAGONIST   168

AUTHOR BIO   170

Jessica Tyner

PART ONE
CHILDHOOD & FAMILY

CHILDHOOD

Two memories from when I was three
define my mother and father. A bath in the chipped
tub bubbling from generous squirts of dish
soap that dried my skin. We could never
afford the real things.
The plastic horse squirt gun, half
full. My father came in
to shave his neck, swiping the blade neatly
around his moustache. When he finished
he turned and scanned my naked body.
I shot him in the face,
scrubbed away his searching eyes and that
is how I learned what a gun is for.
I suckled my mother's breast until I could speak
because she wanted me to. The warm milk
filled my mouth, spreading to my limbs
like a drug. I lay on her chest in their bed,
a cartoon boxing match between a chicken
and a lamb on the TV. They squealed in one ear,
my mother's heart beat in the other. As a bell rang and the animals
began circling, the nipple engorged
against my tongue, grotesque and huge, and that
is when I learned what teeth are for.
Years later, I watched my best friend's
five-year-old daughter
try to cover her mother's
chest with a blanket while her infant brother
was breastfed. A child discovers shame

as quickly as a farm animal
gets the metal bolt to the brain.

Butterfly Storms

I won't feign to know the flight patterns of butterflies.
When I was six my mother gave me an insect catcher,
A Lilliputian tent to trap and confine. Endless summers
I spent roaming our square acre, sprinting after Monarchs

As they jerked like drunkards toward the neon sky. But a tent,
Those can only do so much. Wings make you quick,
So fingers work much better,
Short and grass stained, shining with sweat.

I'd like to believe when I ripped off the orangeblack
Butterfly's wing it was a mistake.
I want to believe it kept soaring high, a little crooked
And only half emptied of grace, untouchable,
Forgetting the stolen wing in my palm,

Or maybe we never forget. Maybe they never forget.

Thirty years later on the California backroads
It came back,
This time in droves, in herds,
Blackened flurries like an anarchic snowstorm. It was the heat
Of summer and still

I barreled through throngs of wings for miles,
Bodies crushed onto windshield, streaks of orange
Amidst the dark. Not once did I stop as the corpses piled up,
Not once did I slow down.

Not once did I falter to look
And breathe in all the destruction I can cause,
All that I'm capable of.

THE SACRAMENT

When I was five I sat with my mother
through the cloying night listening
for the crunch
of his tires gnawing through
gravel. She kept silent,
thumbing the phone,
as I chewed
through piece after piece
of buttered toast and jam,
my gluttony of Eucharist. It was sacred,
our secret,
watchdogs in the dark.

END OF THE HARVEST SEASON

Between the apple trees and past
the pumpkin patch, I rode my Shetland pony
through Farmer Beebe's orchards
down the street. I was five
and my pony a horse, a unicorn,
a hooved goddess on speed.

Together we flew betwixt the fruit
laden towers, my creped thighs
rubbed raw against the leather, straps
burning into my palms,
and in that instant we were whole,
unbroken and alive. Later

in the pasture, her belly thick
with hay and me itching for the wild, again
we cocktailed together, her anger nipping
tighter with each gallop. My beautiful beast
turned sharp, bore down on the iron seesaw.

I learned early what it means
to take a hit, blood and sharp-nosed
pain, lips splitting dark,
an over-ripened harvest. It took years
to try again, to hoist onto her back,
immortal and permanent as a throne. By then,

the years had made me heavy, her shaky and old

so that I might break her back in a cantor,
her athanasia with each stride.

For My Father

Some people have rituals, traditions,
or common sense like hugs and *I love
yous* that are forgotten, but we
had garage sales
on heat-crazed Saturday mornings.
Thirty years later, what I remember
is the "Do you want this?" dipped
slow in a thick Oklahoma drawl
as you raised a one-dollar-stickered
ceramic horse with your callused
brown hands. The tough pancakes
from McDonald's suffocating
in syrup. Driving for miles, following
cardboard signs, reading directions
to you from the Nickel ads, fingers
black and grimy.
I don't remember your face
at my piano recitals or your words
on my birthday. But I'll always know
how thin your legs looked wrapped
in jeans next to mine in the truck,
the country song you sang
to make me roll my eyes,
and how good the endless
coke and peanuts tasted
that Mom never would have let me
have, the salt blanketing my thighs
like a secret gathering dust.

Passing

I was twelve before I realized
my father wasn't white.
Until then I thought nothing
of his clay-colored skin, eyes dripping
like honey, or ropes of black licorice hair
snaking, alive and furious, down his back.
My breasts sprung early, hips splayed
wide as an overeager invitation
with bones pushing unforgiving
against my own skin, pale and quiet
as the illness. You took me to Radio Shack,
your syrupy southern drawl wrapping like a shy gift
around the simple words,
My wife put something on hold,
and the young clerk, not a decade older than me,
looked at both of us with blatant disgust—
loathing, a shot of envy
even. I could sniff it out, like a dog
or a wild thing.
Is this your wife? the clerk asked, and my chest
was in a painful awakening of an instant
freakishly large, my hips
unable to slam shut, and my father,
too stunned to be ashamed or angered, just whispered,
That's my daughter, before walking out, the snakes gone still.
But for the years I'm too sorry to take back,
the years until the cancer sucked you dry,
I felt it for both of us,

felt it in my thighs built like a horse
and my lips too ripe for a child,
in every year after labor-heavy year,
I refused to be seen with you. I'm so sorry
that I saw you gut-punched and ugly as a man..

To the Bone

I'm sure I don't remember this right—it's not
How the human body is made. At fifteen, I ran
Like Oonawieh Unggi through the dark, hiding in the bushes,
Curled into their collapsing limbs in the backyard—past the horse
pasture,
Beyond the overgrown vegetable garden,
Teenagers playing hide-and-seek among the crumbling barn
And old, weeping garage. Home
Was in the makeshift bar out back,
The one my father built for my mother during the hoping years.
With your gait gaining on me, wind knotting my hair,
I didn't know then what really chased me. All I knew
Was that I had to get home, to the false security
Of the musty old bar. When my hand smashed

Through the ancient glass door, shards spewing
Like a comet through the dark,
The pain was nowhere, spit out in the drooling blood
And the missing skin from my arm,
Stripped like onion peels and dropped on the floor,
Cold to the touch. I swear to God
I could see straight to the bone, white
As lunula and shining like a trophy.

Decades later I'm still asked by strangers
Why I tried to kill myself, their eyes wide and wishing
For some wild story marinated in angst. And every time,
Every time,

I say the same thing I did at fifteen:
If I wanted to kill myself I wouldn't cut myself up
Like a kindergarten's palm-finger turkey.
It would be tight, clean, flawless lines,
Not this,

This garish showcasing of scars
Worn like a dried corsage around my wrist.

THE MEATWORKS

Shepherded to the slaughterhouse, I was sixteen,
Dumb and easily lured from the mob. At midnight,
We soared across state lines, pregnant with the thrill
Of it all, young Stockholmers watching for cruisers
And finally

Before the sun broke over the 97, with Redmond
Still stretched out beyond the barbs
A white wolf stood lone and grand on the median
Surveying the highway, the escapees
 From the night. My warden's eyes arrested mine

And he let me go.

I never went home again,
Reveling in being hunted down,
The stupid prey,
Holding tight the hand
That led me to my abattoir.

Two Days Prior to the Burial

twenty-some years and all i have is one memory
 of you—well, maybe not one, but one collection
that is the same
the same
with different places and people but we just kept
acting them out over and over
remember
all those times the waiters thought you were Mexican
(my skin being so much whiter than yours—white
like hospital linens or the deepest center of stargazer lilies)
¿Qué te gusta comer?
but more than that
i remember the downcast gaze of your eyes
shoulders curved in like damp heavy wings
jaw twitching beneath masseter in that way all men have
of showing pain
hurt
fear
humiliation
no more shattered ashtrays
splintered cue sticks
urine-soaked
closets
i don't miss you
(sometimes quietly i miss
what i wish you had been)
i miss
your strong white teeth

before the chemo ate your bones down to nail-thin shaven peels
i miss the decade
before i found out you didn't meet her
at a friend's party
but through her prison writings
memory forgive me
I miss
your accent
when I hear it in my voice say
eugene
guitar
fuchsia
i miss the days
when i didn't notice the difference in our skin
i miss the nights
you made me brown cows milky streams
licking down the glass

PART TWO
COSTA RICA

SPELEOLOGY

Ocean water began chewing and spitting
out what became the Venado Caves thirty
million years ago, almost as long
as I've loved you. Guatusos aborigines were first
to slice their slim perfect limbs
through the dark, sliding callused fingers
against the jaw fossils of humpback whales
trapped in a scream along the caverns.
Caves don't swallow people is a lie
slipped through swollen brown lips
and I'm supposed to be grateful
to be one of the first people to crawl
on hands and knees
through bat guano while the little beasts
beat their wings, furious and terrified
above me. This is what I've done
for you. Felt the brush
of tarantula legs
on my thigh, the sickening crush
of a bloated cockroach under my palm,
completely unseeing and reaching
for whatever might reach back.
There's no light at the end of the tunnel.
Everything circles back to where it began,
and for one long minute I have to stand
between the splayed legs
of what should have stayed buried at sea
so my eyes don't burst into blindness
from the sheer brightness of it all.

En Moravia

You're in tico's eyes, the plumpness
of Ricardo's lips, the trapped heat of strange
men's coiled hair overgrown as *mangas*. The equator
sun doesn't fade memories,
instead,
the heat pulls your scent out of young
boy's underarms. The rain clings tight everything
I'm trying to forget. Every day
on *Ruta* 43, I count *colones* into old men's hands
as browned and faithless as yours.

The Carving Station

Miguel fed me sips of whiskey as he stitched
a nadie te pareces desde que yo te amo
across my rib cage in between
moles and scars and halting English,
discarded fragments of the cancer.
In the undergrad days,
my professor told me to always, always
have beautiful words—
other than your own—
running through your head.
You don't want to wake up
locked in solitary confinement alone.
Every day comes in the end.
The malignancy is the shackles, you
were the padded walls
and a Chilean poet was my grasping hope
escaped from my slipping mind,
a pedestal beneath carved breasts.

Pinky Swears and Kitchen Chairs

We were sure we wouldn't live to thirty, to hell
with whether we wanted to or not.
Rosalind hung herself a week after her brother wove
his own noose. Two Catholic funerals
in two weeks was more suffocating
than the sick collecting
above their kicked out chairs.
We all would have been twenty-eight,
but Sheri left a decade before, spine snapped
underneath a four wheeler in a plowed
field. She should have been in seventh
period with us, but you know how kids are.
The day I turned thirty, I jumped from a groaning bridge
somewhere deep
in the jungles of Central America. Village children
clung to the edge with bugged eyes
and flurries of Spanish splitting their lips.
Somewhere between feeling nothing
beneath my feet and mouthfuls of regrets
I knew the cord would snap,
and when it didn't
I was swarmed with the stinging knowing
that I had been forgotten even by death
and probably had been for decades.

Holy Week at Playa Negra

In patchwork Spanish, I bought us
two bus tickets to Puerto Viejo.
For five hours, a woman's dreadlocks
sketched elaborate maps
into sweat that buttered my forearm
every time she slipped her baby
upside down to change a diaper
with the grace and instinct
of a dancer. The black sand
burned through my feet while you taught me
how to catch a wave. You have to wait
for the perfect one, swelling
like leaking breasts, diving
into the underbelly and slicing
through to the calm.
I've never been good
at waiting or ducking, what a heartbreak
to miss the crash. The ocean floor
devoured my face, ate into a cheek,
and filled my throat
with burning salt water.
On the way back to the hotel,
you held my hand and I wished
that it was his, oversized and hungry.
A sinewy man carved a coconut
with a machete
as carefully as a skilled lover
undresses their darling.

Sand is made from defeated
rocks, bones of fish,
and I wanted nothing more
than to drink down my shame
with that bowed-back man's
sunwarm milk.

Love You More

I sent you a keychain stamped *love
you more* from my crumbling
Costa Rican hacienda. You
were turning thirty and we
had years of regrets stitched
and scarred up and down
our arms like teenagers
in the grip of delusion, tired dogs
after the fights.
I waited
until you caught up with me
to say I was coming back,
my muscles tensed,
fat scars ropy thick, ready
for a blossoming explosion
black as your eyes swimming
beneath heavy brow,
and deafening as your lips wrapped
like a vise around my name.

Inside the Rosemary Bush

Early in the morning, while the tea is steeping,
I put out the ashtray full of seeds and bread
crusts for the *quetzels* and *yigüirros*.
The rosemary bush shakes underneath
the clothes I forgot to bring in from the line,
little fat brown balls roll out
who have no shortage
of food, no predators, a backyard in Moravia
all to themselves. Their water pump to bathe
in, the cas tree dropping sweets
at their feet. This is what I left you for.
Watching overstuffed birds,
beggars tapping at the gates calling upe!
the huevos man barking prices from a rusted van,
while I sit and write
page after page about you.

leave two pounds of skin

the love cries of the cicadas
smothered the grunts of shuddering buses
bursts of spanish from ticos buying la nacion
and guanabana fruits
on the street corner
the sure snap of the straps
as the nurses tied me down
arms splayed
crucified like a cat
about to be spayed
respirar profundo roberto says
slipping the rubbery mask
over my scrubbed down face
and I suck deep
gas gropes my insides
exploring every lobe
the determined chorus belts
from guanacaste trees below
imago's tymbal membranes contracting
buckling muscles clicking in
clicking out
air sacs in abdominal chambers
keening for their mates
the nymph claws and climbs
up through dirt
with instinct and strong legs
after years in the dark
under the ungodly brightness

of the equator sun
molting for the last time a skeleton
of what was clings to the bark
nakedly fragile and discarded
as wednesday morning trash

The Road Past Cartago

I drove to Irazu Volcano two weeks
after being split open and threaded
back together. The lurching station
wagon barely made it up the curling
road. Villagers hung their fresh
laundry in the fields, stained underwear
and baby bibs slapping in the breeze
among the smell of morning
gallo pinto and cow manure.
At the highest point,
I parked the choking
car and walked toward the crater,
ash and sand crawling
between my toes, stitches pulling tight
in my stomach. There are no guards
en paraiso, no insurmountable fences,
no signs telling you no.
Ducking under the broken
wooden gate, I witnessed the abyss
below. Sulfur makes Diego de la Haya
turquoise as a cartoon and I
crouched down like a child,
pressed my palm hard into the heat
of a wound that blossomed
as effortlessly as a *Guaria Morada*,
as beautifully as the last eruption,
and wished you were there.

THE CATAMARAN

May's long weekend was spent
on a catamaran in Manuel Antonio,
the crew's thick Jamaican tongues
twisting around tico Spanish.
On the upper deck,
I said I was leaving you
and couldn't look you in the face.
A dolphin laughed
and an Indian couple on their honeymoon
asked you to take their picture.
For three hours, you tried
to untangle my reasons
until we both grew seasick
and spent the sunset hanging
our heads over the rails.

The Banana Plantation

Roberto passed a joint to me with sand-ploughed fingers
in the jungles miles above Limon while the others
did headstands inside between sips of wine
and rum from their bottles. Nobody talked
to Roberto. He was so beautiful
he stole your voice.
I didn't want to kiss him, I wanted
to memorize how he shook shells
as small as pinky nails from his dreads
and how his hip bones protruded like fins. *My father
says that the ocean will swallow
me one day,* he said. The woven hammock
chewed into my bare thighs while he perched
like a kingfisher on the porch rail
and told me how he worked
his father's banana plantation every morning.
The smoke filled my head as he rocked
me gently, golden fist around hammock knots,
thick accent stumbling around foreign words
and all I could picture between his rolling r's
was the sunrise
surfing ritual, pink slipping from sky,
how his chest was chiseled
stone from the breakers,
how the saltwater rutted
into him, shining off his shoulders,
even when the waters let him go, even
when his feet thrust into old Nikes,

even when it was time to weave
between the bushes, slipping
plastic soda sacks over one
banana bunch after another.

PART THREE
THE MIDDLE EAST

CALL TO PRAYER

Sick with fever in Abu Dhabi, I curled
retching in his empty bed like a cat
hell-bent on grooming myself
out of existence, throat hairy and tongue
thick as a pregnant fig. Across the sand-coated street,
an oil-black man crept across a rooftop,
 one inch tall and limbs strong as ropes,
to rub and knead and love another perfect
window frame on another perfect villa
swollen with gaud and waste. If I could dredge up the strength,
I'd have pulled that damp t-shirt with its sucking threads
over my sweat-knotted hair,
pushed your weary boxers
down my hips, bones protruding like coat hangers,
and pressed my bare breasts against the window,
hot as a frying pan, my gift,
my offering, to that sinewy miniature man
as the sun tore through his skin. The loudspeaker
from the mosque down the street
blared the third call to prayer, making the men
march like wind-up soldiers, mats cradled
like tired children in their arms.

I Thought You Were Praying

Driving madly through the deserts outside Al Ain,
the baby sucking like a beast at your breast,
mosques gave way to dunes
and the Paki street workers to palms.
Beyond the camels,
beyond the tribesmen,
we didn't stop until we were away from it all—
the malls with their ungodly air conditioning,
the fat children making loud love to their sweets,
the fat wives engorged in their abayas, rolling
like sun-swollen beetles through the shops.
In ballet flats and the jeans that hugged my ass
like a fetish, I climbed the dunes as if I belonged,
while beautiful golden men in glorious keffiyehs
honked safely from the highway. And I,
staggering like a drunk
as the dune clung—begging and desperate,
my cuckolded lover—to my perfect white feet,
mounted the crest, dropped to my knees,
ready and eager as a whore,
and filled a mason jar with contraband. And you,
nipples burnished as the sand, laughed,
I thought you were praying.

Racing Camels

Three women drove the Black Mambo
through the panting morning fog of Abu Dhabi,
dodging the Ferraris and Lamborghinis, the busses
tipped upside down and teeming with bloody workers
along the banks thick with red sand
blown in like bullets from the dunes.
We wanted to see the camel race.
On the outskirts of Al Wathba, young Arabs gathered at dawn,
urging their animals on, praying for the speed and heart
to catch the eye of the Sheikh, get a piece of themselves
tucked like another pretty bar of gold into the palace.
We were the only foreigners there,
we were the only women there
when the fog eased, an expert dom releasing his sub,
seconds before the asphyxiation left a lasting mark
and the camels,
the camels,
they say they run for Allah, white spittle
soaping their mouths, but my God how they're ugly:
legs too long and spindly to carry their bodies,
all knobby knees and wavering humps
like they don't know their own carriage,
like fourteen-year-old girls—
and in that they're suddenly beautiful.
The camels run with a deity's grace
and it doesn't matter that their bellies are thick
or their lips lift in the wind, baring crooked teeth
to the desert. We snaked along the tracks,

pacing the loping streaks until an old man wearing a hard face,
 dishdash gritty with the sport, keffiyeh fighting the winds,
pulled alongside us. We weren't supposed to be here,
but then again
the camels aren't supposed to know elegance,
to defy their bodies, to move like gods,
and so I waved to the Emirati, and in an instant
his hardness cracked, his hand lifted
and he burst into a smile bright enough to blow
the lingering gray from the sky.

SOMETHING SWEET

Do you want something sweet?
Your toddler came at me like a bacchanal,
Mouth open with desire. Imagine
Being that trusting, certain
That what was placed on your tongue would please,
Sugar grains scrubbing down your palate,
Ghee melting like perfection down your throat.

Kadri didn't know I called the *besan ladoo* sandballs,
That they required the perfect mix of chickpea
And *kadalai maavu*, that the *elachi* was the secret,
Or that you had to sieve the flour just right. All he knew

Was that sweet was something good, that hands
Were made for his pleasures. Imagine
Knowing that naiveté, the undoubting innocence

When spreading your lips wide.

PART FOUR
THE SELF

SAVAGERY

What are you? I can see
The Indian in your cheekbones.
My skin, white as the albumin
On salmon, the only whisper of Cherokee
Etched into the bones begging to be birthed.
Show me your tribal card,
Your ancestry lineage, proof
Of Dawes Rolls in your blood.
Am I not Native enough for you?

You look like something. Something
Savage and uncontained.

OUTSIDE THE BOXING GYM

A fist to the face is a glorious thing. First,

Time freezes, muscles tensed for the strike,
A hook from a boxer
Is wholly unlike
hooking a fish, no sharpness, no blood,

It soaks into your bones
As hot butter on bread, shakes your brain loose
And then settles again, slightly off kilter,

Not with a glove, and not with hands wrapped,
With no points being given or combinations on deck,
No fighting back or praying for bells—gorgeous
In simplicity, unbearably still.

I'm asking you to hit me
hard as you can, I said quick.
To the boy buried deep beneath brawn.
 Twice my size, swing away
and carry me home.

HOW I LIKE MY WOMEN

I like my women slight and frail, bones
Hollowly light, ribcages pressed
Like prison bars against the skin.
I love the women with stomachs caved in,
Divots carved like ice cream scoops
Below breasts begging to melt. It's the women
With the lips like readied blisters, skin sautéed
In good genes and creams
That remind me how exquisite we are
And of all I'll never be.

The Lecture

You think I want to be here?
Listen, I was young like you once, too. I thought
of traveling the world and I did a little and let me tell you

there's nothing romantic about drunken Korean men
vomiting on your shoes in the subway or the Ticos on the beaches
holding your hand and sucking down iced sodas poured in plastic bags
while they give thirteen-year-old local girls the up and down.

Just listen to me. I wanted to go to Iowa. I stood
on the murderous barstools at the Yamhill Pub on open mic night
and told roomfuls of drunken strangers about my one-night stands.
I read the Bell Jar and fancied myself Esther
or thought, you know, if I'd just been born in the right decade
they'd have called me more handsome than Marlon Brando
and I could've been drunk every night

or crafted the perfect suicide letter. Listen,
I've done all that and let me tell you something you already know,

that thing that keeps tapping at your brain when you wake up at four
in the morning,
it's already started to slip away and you'd better pray,
you'd better pray,
that you at least had the foresight during one of those late nights
when you were wrapping your legs around someone who's face you
don't remember

or who's face is just too ridiculously familiar now that you at least did
something—

something—
to make damn sure that there's something waiting for you on the
other end
because if there's not, if you didn't think you'd get old like me,
like all the rest of us,
that's not going to stop the freight train that's headed straight toward
you

and it's going to smash the living hell out of you because it can,
because it doesn't care, because that's its nature
and just like you it will roll right over something someone at some
time considered precious
and barely even wonder what that bump was as it keeps on screaming
into the night.

BOUQUET OF THE BODY

What they don't tell you about starvation
is that you hunger for nothing.
The pounds drop, an exhausted mother
letting go of a wailing newborn. Inches
slough away, callouses and tired skin
pumiced off with a burning stone.
I never once felt empty.
Instead, my stomach grew tauter,
crescent arrangements wilting beneath eyes
bruised and battered as wedding day gardenias,
buried in creams and powders,
and my hip bones blossomed,
a quiet display of Asiatic lilies,
sickeningly sweet and nearly weeping
before the decay set in.

Genetically Isolated Since the Ice Age

I starved myself the wrong way
not with a wailing stomach and day-long naps
but with the kind of hunger you reserve for pure hatred
(or fear)
I was an animal
 gutting turkeys and chewing through the cow's gristle
pushing through bags of raw vegetables and passing
on all the offers of sweet whiskey, the good bread puddings
and perfect gin martinis with perfect slices of ice
that had kept me warm and fat
bundled in thick layers of subcutaneous blubber
for all those lonely years
I hadn't sprung up like a flower
and I didn't wither like one, either, not me,
for me, it was the failing predator's way
a flailing Kodiak bear
dragging a rusted trap in my wake so you can all see where I've been
until the starvation caught me
tackled me to the earth and I breathed in the musk
of where we're all going
the embrace turning more tender
as the weight sloughed off until all that's left
is a solid block of sharp bones wrapped tight
in a fancy pantsuit of new muscle so young
and so shiny
and so utterly unlike who I am
or who I thought I was
I don't know how to wear it right

and it's just so painfully
heartbreakingly obvious
I'm playing dress-up in a closet
I don't belong

On the Runway

Tell me I'm svelte, tell me I'm thin,
that my walk is defectless, limb after limb,
that my cheekbones are just the right
daggering peaks, not too Cherokee, just barely
a shadowed half breed, that my shoulders roll back
quite effortlessly,
yet not from a decade of Camels
and Wheel, but a bend born
of nature, genetic lotteries, still
that my chest rises grandly as foam on the tide
my starvation was worth it,
this swaggering stride.

BATTLE SCARS

I pulled myself out of the brambles
The same way I flung myself in, coating
The scratches with saliva, ignoring the thorns
Stabbing like satisfying hunger pangs
Into my disappearing flesh.
There was no intervention, no dramatic
Segue into rehab. I enlisted headfirst,
Discharged in shame, sheepish
And dazed from the fights. After a war, soldiers
Can say, with pride, they fought for their country,
For freedom,
For peace. But in the aftermath
Of the war with the self, there's no pride,
No glory. Just the battle scars of a heart
That began to fail, the tissue-fine skin
With no meat to cling to and the knowing
That I can let my body consume itself
While I sit back, the silent, stupid onlooker
And watch the troop's parade roll by.

"Eating Like a Bird, It's Really a Falsity"
—Norman Bates

You don't just decide to start eating again, it happens slow,
a groggy crawl and stumble out of a dream.
I didn't choose to starve myself,
I didn't choose to stop. It was a cycle, my own metamorphosis
full of Kafka leanings and sopping new wings.
Built up like an orgasm, I can't tell you
the foreplay, the spots touched that got me there,
the details of the teasing
or the fetishes reveled in (that's sacred),
but I can tell you this: I woke up
in Washington Park, stomping the trails behind the zoo.
Maybe it was the humbling houses of the West Hills,
or the reservoirs spreading like spilt champagne
at my feet, but on that day
I woke with a start. Past the rose garden poached
with pale tourists, past the fountain where droplets sound like church
bells,
I climbed to the playground at the top of the hill,
slipped onto a swing and learned
all over again
how easy it is to fly. It's a lovely thing
to face your fragility and still take flight. But birds,
"birds really eat a tremendous lot," so give me the fat ones,
the thick ones, the ones burrowed down deep,
fill me with their earthiness until I choke from the grit,
desperate for air, neck arching and jaw flexing,
bones slight and delicate as a song.

PART FIVE

LOVE (THE EARLY YEARS)

Choreography

To follow in dance is to have a conversation,
Albeit often one of the sexually laced variety,
The kind made in hushed corners of bars between
Sips of gin and sweetened breaths—the kind
Leading to a crescendo of fingertips
Pressed into thighs and loose kisses
In bathrooms or taxis I'll forget by morning,
But to lead,
That's giving a persuasive speech,
A manifesto of sorts, oily words slipped
Between practiced smiles, a litany
Masked as a spoonful of something
That's supposed to be good for us,
And I,
I've never been good at politics.
So let me just follow, match
My body to yours and we can both pretend
It's all for the sake of a rhythm and rules
Written hundreds of years ago,
An excuse
To do as the beasts do.

How to Oil an Indian Man's Hair

Your apartment smells like coconut oil
in the mornings. Watch the Vatika bottle
spin lazy circles in the microwave to be sure
it doesn't melt. You sit between my legs,
your dry naked feet crossed and me
perched like a fragile, cautious bird
on the buttery leather couch. Pull over the cheap
dark square table, fold a paper napkin twice,
pour the milky warm oil into my palm,
place the bottle on the napkin.
I wear nothing but your boxer shorts,
your low tsk tsk as the oil slips
through my thin fingers, burrows between bones,
falls onto pallid thighs white as flashes
against your skin. Begin at your scalp,
rub it in. Add more oil, finger comb
your long black hair,
curling, waking snakes unwinding down your back.
Take off your glasses, thumb your temples. I'm greased
as a dirty dog to my elbows. Stop, wait,
still for your giant perfect hands
(puppy hands, my janu)
to swallow mine easily as a cobra. You
smelled like coconuts
cracked open
letting all the sweetness out.

THE

First time I tasted you
I suffocated in your cologne,
flailing desperate
over your nicotine-laced tongue,
second time around you kneaded my thighs
white as unbaked fry bread
until I slapped your hand,
three months together bred nothing
but teeth marks and swollen eyes,
last year before I left
we pretended everything could keep
going on like it was,
final night together you cried
between my legs while I finger
combed your hair and told myself
it was worth it..

THINGS MAHAVIRA DOESN'T KNOW

As a child, I saw a cartoon of a devout man
endlessly whisking a broom before his steps
so that he would not crush an insect
never thinking that the man was real
or that the broom wouldn't save me.
Your lips weren't made to know flesh
but they memorized my body,
every flaw and spark.
 Gujarati prayers slipped
over nimble tongue and crowded teeth
night after stumbling night
before you whispered that my thighs
were as fair as the milk
you boiled and spooned
into my mouth.

CHRISTMAS CHAI

For Christmas I gave you an aphotic
steel teapot and you taught me
how to make chai.
I filled the gaping vessel's mouth with tap water
while you peeled slices of unwashed
ginger root. Two spoons
of Taj Mahal ground tea, a mouthful
for each.
Cardamom pods, cracked with your crooked teeth
and pried open with fingernails, tossed
helpless in the boil. Milk
comes last,
an opaque white stream
soothing dark spiced water.
The sweetness we could never agree on—
my slow honey, your raw
sugar. That Christmas you gave me words wrapped
in a lilting accent and I taught you
how to say I love you.
I opened my mouth to take you in
while you peeled away clothes from the night
before to spoon,
together, on the mattress.
You bit my shoulder, red fissures from teeth
while I pulled your frenzied hair. Lost together
in the cheap red sheets,
I never came last.
And the sweetness
we could never agree on.

Anatomy of a Trunk

Our first Christmas
you agreed to pick out a tree
from an ice-glazed farm
in the outskirts of Portland.
Frozen mud, a tiny barn
filled with ornaments and honey sticks,
and you. Walking the acres,
frost cracking beneath weathered boots,
you pointed to a sturdy blue spruce
and clutched a cigarette in one hand,
me in the other,
while the down-cloaked cowboy
fingered awake the birth cries
of his chainsaw. Squealing
like an animal at slaughter, starving
steel teeth bit into the periderm,
brown sap-soaked flesh flying.
The bone-white secondary phloem exposed,
undressed and naked in winter grays,
the saw masticated wildly
into the vascular rays, slicing effortless
through growth rings
and into the heart wood. Your
fingers wove through mine, filling
each palm line with warmth,
every mound with memory
as our tree fell soft,
defeated and dying in the pasture.

EATING

A man makes love the way he eats. You
always devoured the *daal*
like a starving animal, thick fingers
yellowed with turmeric pinching
the steaming naan, over-ripened
lips slick with the juices of burst
lentils. Afterward, you did the same
to me, tearing at my flesh, hungry
and never sated. For years,
I watched you suck and lap
up everything laid before you
and I realized I would never be
enough to satisfy you.

LIMITS OF THE TONGUE

You always had the habit
of devouring with relish everything
that fit between your lips.
Ten thousand buds can never
blossom wide enough
to satisfy the cravings
of my skin,
the sweet rawness
behind knees, the salt
of my collar bone. Taste me
like a Mumbai robber fly,
with every line of your body,
from the soles of your feet
to the swell of your mouth,
juices running like burst kamrak
fruit, overripe and heavy.

Drag Me Through the Mess

Love stories aren't tidy and wrapped up in ribbons—
at least not ours
and that's how I like it. Drag me

through the mess, the neuroses pressed into your brain
by the hands that wove your childhood jalebi
and tell me something nice
that makes me feel pretty, something

crafted with nuances and peppered
with subtleties that neither of us fully believe,
but the lies so sweet and drenched in syrupy half-
truths

neither of us can help but binge on the gluttony,
engorging ourselves on one another.

The Last Exotic Petting Zoo

In the dripping cold of an Oregon January,
miasma of wet dog clung to us like a
discarded lover. You, sick
with a cough, a heavy head tucked
into the pages of a book. I drove
like hell down the coastal
back roads. No one holds tigers
and lions in the winter
but us.
The wanton mud swallowed our shoes,
sucked our feet in searching gulps
while the animals watched.
You held her,
bristled paws like a kiwano,
as I cradled the bottle of milk
into her frantic mouth
knowing you'll never
think me as magnificent as you
do right now.
 I gifted you a tiger cub, her claws etching
delicate scars into your forearms,
while the rain scoured us to the bone.

RECIPE FOR MOONG DAAL

Look at me like you did
the first time you made me moong daal,
my Otis Redding and Eartha Kitt,
uncertain in the tiny, dirty kitchen
and you, oiled black ringlets
falling like madmen on your brow.
Press me hard against the counter,
knead your hands
into my waist, trace your fingers
over hip bones,
invade my mouth with yours
between the squealing whistles
of the pressure cooker.
Oil heating in the saucepan, dusted
with cumin seeds,
watch them struggle until they're the same
soft brown as your hairless arms
pulling me close, between the stove
and you. We tear dried red
chilies into the pan, adding the spice.
Dice slick green peppers
on a makeshift cutting board, thick
fingers deftly working the small,
fragile slivers with the same certainty
they handle me. Grate in ginger root
with rhythmic practice, add the curry leaves.
Onions and turmeric are next
as I lean against the refrigerator,

breathing you in, the scent of your sweat
with the bite of red onions.
Grab me tight, taste my neck
while the turmeric spreads golden
in the hiss. A pinch of *asafoetida*,
all the pan holds poured into the cooker
and for ten minutes you deconstruct
me, long ginger-scented fingers
stained yellow brushing my lips,
black onion-teary eyes searching
and the blues
crying like forgotten children.

THE PHOTOGRAPH

When I asked to see a photo of your parents
it was to gauge my enemy, the people
who had a neat row of women lined up
for you in Mumbai, who would turn
you away if they ever knew the color
of my skin or my American name. I wanted
to see you in them, a shadow
of your brimming over lips,
if your mother's eyes were opaque
ink blots like yours, if your father's
cruelty was palpable
through the film. What you showed me
was an aging couple, shoulders
hugging in like damp wings.
Your mother
was blowing out her birthday candles
and there was nothing
of you in them.

Symptoms of an End

Let me take you back to the Red Woods
where we drank cup after cup
of Dutch Brother's hazelnut coffee,
sucked the flesh from fish bones,
salty oysters from their homes.
I'd drive you again
over the state line,
my hand on your thick thigh
while the Oregon pines shake
with uncertainty
as if they don't realize
how incredible they are,
and you ask your empty hands,
Aren't these trees big enough?

Night Before Mumbai

The night before you returned to Mumbai
we ducked through an Oregon downpour,
cradling gifts for your family: knee braces
for your grandfather,
chocolate wafers for cousins,
a pink baby doll that closed her eyes
for the youngest. I had left the oven on
in my tiny one-room basement apartment,
the baking heat dry
and suffocating as India
melted the butterscotch chips
in our hands, soft and golden
on your skin.
 You kissed me in the crowded kitchen,
sticky fingers undressed me,
devoured me
with the same relish you gave everything
you swallowed greedy as a child.
I was your first taste
of buttered tilapia,
warm slivers of flesh and juices
ran down chins, an aged
scotch held at the back of tongues,
unfolding flavors, the drying slicks
of yellow sweets licked from a collar
bone. You were always too hungry for me
to ever fill you up.

Bronco Busting

The years whipped strap burns through my fingers,
gnawing on slippery palms as I scrambled
to tie-down rope you,
a cowboy cinching a calf's noose.
We were in Pendleton,
the last stop on a lifetime of pulling leather.
You bought me a Stetson and snapped
roll after roll as the Indians strapped
on paper numbers and feathers,
dancing for the white crowds.
You,
 above my huckleberry, I thought impossible
to break—
clove-hitched to my post
as I slipped hobbles over your boots
in our heat-soaked boom town,
manure cloying as a perfume.

For the Animals

A horse's heart weighs more than you'd think.
Make them work for it,
the keeper said,
so I hid the organs and quartered head pieces
around the sagging chamber,
a macabre and ridiculous game.
But the cold heart I placed prominently,
with a sickening wet slap,
on the apex of the slab. And the lions roared,
a gut crushing, ancient wail
while I grappled with thigh meat,
velvet nostrils and black searching eyes,
and the lions didn't care,
foaming with want, restless
like I was for you for all those years.
She licked the shoulder to the bone
with a blood-stained lipsticked muzzle
while he worked teeth through hair
coarse as untended pubic down
no fingers would claw, rake, or search
but the cubs—
still young enough to share a ribcage
that took two of us to carry—
ignored the carnage and stared me to stillness, ticking off
the last day of my cycle.
They can smell me,
crouching beside them,
heat with slivers of copper,

thick and heady between my legs.
They were too stupidly new to do anything
but notice, watch and wonder at me—
paws as absurdly oversized and dangerous as yours—
me with my too-thin legs wrapped in tired denim
and spread like an afterthought of an offering
only for the animals.

A Wednesday Afternoon

Come back home tired from the commute,
your badge forgotten around your neck and slide
into your cushion on the good couch,
the one we picked out together. Let's watch
the ridiculous people on the ridiculously expensive TV,
cook ridiculously exquisite food while we hunker
over hot boxes from Whole Foods and after,
only after,
let's lie in the position every set of lovers calls their own,
your erection pressing tight against your shorts,
my head buried deep and hot into the crevice of your torso
and even though my tongue is still too stupid and stumbling, even
after all these years,
all I want to do is tilt my head up and tell you
while you begin to breathe the breath of the sleeping
just how goddamned beautiful you look.

VALENTINE'S DAY

That Valentine's Day I carried a fever back
from the Middle East and we skipped the dinner,
passed on the ballet
and instead you brought me peonies
wrapped like submissives in twine and butcher paper.
For hours, you sat beside me,
wiping my burning face with an iced washcloth
while I slipped in and out of sleep, dreaming
one nightmare after another.
And it was glorious
without the heels,
without the suit,
without the perfumes and makeup and valet
to spend the night battling monsters
until I clenched my teeth and cried so hard
I bit clean through the mercury.

FILTHY TIGER CHAI SOAP

That headache clung like a teething child
Every morning I awoke in New York,
And the Hindi filled my mouth—
Thick and blundering as an elephant calf—
But still I pushed on.
Boy, Ladkaa,
Where is he, Vo kahaa hai,
All gone, Sub khatum.
I wandered the boroughs for miles,
Wore my boots down to dust,
Dug up hangnails and ground my bones
To dull, aching pulses looking in vain
For something you'd adore. Something
That would bring me home.
It was in Greenwich Village, betwixt
Noosed ropes of necklaces and rings
Made from typewriter keys where I found it:
Filthy tiger chai soap, a tiny square
Of fat and spices
Shipped from somewhere as foreign
And beautiful as you,
Somewhere so far away and alien
That the words to take me back,
Home, ghar,
Stuck fast and thick
Like dry roti in my throat. I choked
On the perfectness of it all, teeth
Biting quick, jaw locking tight.

I was an animal, I was the tiger,
Sloping hunched and silent
And mad with hunger.

The Salt Lick

choose me
like i chose you all those years ago
like we chose to spend that weekend
at the bottom of a lake that dried up
fourteen thousand years past somewhere
between utah and nevada
mountain and pacific
temples and brothels
god
and the ungodly
we drove since dawn just to see the salt flats
and then afterward
after the boise police searched the car for marijuana
and found a fixed blade instead
after the disappointing diners
and the ice cream shaped like baked potatoes
after the porn-ridden hotel room
with the mirrors on the ceiling
we tucked our heads down in a truck stop cantina
heavy horses with heavy feedbags
one chili relleno after another
i felt the heat in my throat and the slick on my lips
but i just kept tasting the salt
of when i'd pretended i didn't notice you
taking photo after photo on the flats
of me barefoot bending and licking
the brittle white salt
from that prehistoric lake

Inside the Devil's Punch Bowl

What makes up the cocktail of the Devil's Punch Bowl?
On that long rain-whipped weekend, it was a day of overpriced paella,
Sticky saltwater taffy, and burned espresso.
Do you want to just go? But no,
We trudged on.

Scramble down the steps and you'll emerge
A sorry Venus on the beach.
We've made all the memories here we can. That's wrong,
There's always more.

Clamor over the rock where no one goes,
Where the tide sneaks in quick as a bandit,
A shallow cove full of ancient things
And cigarette butts. What is that?
Is it alive?

On a holiday weekend, hundreds wrapped their raincoats
Tighter around thick bellies,
But we've never done like the rest, and here,
This is our reward: a baby seal lion,
The size of a football, glorious and alone.

It barked and cried, too small to move—I know
How it feels. Abandoned or a mother gone fishing,
We'll never know, but we stayed
Until the tide came in, until the cub was too tired
To hold open its squid-ink eyes, until blind trust

Was the only option—and we left it,

A tiny saint facing down the ocean.

How Dying is Done

They always tell you it's like a cancer, horse piss
spearing thick as butter into perfect alabaster,
but it's not like that at all.
When the black sickness began to crawl
up my arm, claws
dug in deep, inching up forearms
wrapped tight in veins.
The paramedics and nurses and doctors were right,
It did look like cancer
if cancer had the vanity
to primp and preen in the ugly
morning light, but cancer,
it has more modesty
or shame than that. I watched it spread,
arching and keening like a crazed lover
while the doctors filed in, pudgy, tired penguins
telling me time and again
We don't know what this is, but this,
this is how dying is done.

We'll cut off the arm
To save the head and heart.
I'd heard that before,
year after knife-twisting year,
but an amputation doesn't stop it.
Cuts aren't clean,
no matter who's wielding the scalpel.
God, I waited for the clichés, for the lights

or the montage or the regrets
to pour in as the monsoon,
but that's not how dying is done.

You keep on wanting
what your heart's been suffocating,
bearing down underneath blood and muscle—but still
It refuses to drown—what your head
turns away from, holding up ridiculous
mobiles and distractions that even a child
wouldn't fall for. You.

You were what I wanted
when the darkness set in, so furious and real
that it refused to stay buried like a guilt-soaked
secret. We'd grown into something so much heavier,
something of such Botero grandiosity,
that not even a vehicle as strong as my body
could keep it quiet or stop it from bursting into blossom.

OF TRANS AMS AND CHICKENS

My old '83 Trans Am lapped up the salted highway,
clear stripper shoes in the backseat and fried chicken
pressed against my thigh. There was nothing special
about that day, nothing different about the bruises
creeping up my shins to rest uncomfortably on my knees—
backpackers breaking on a pointed rock, wiping sweat on their ascent—
nothing changed about the black Knightrider Hot Wheels hanging
from the rearview mirror or the worn wooly seat covers
molded perfectly to my ass.
I don't know what made me think of you,
what wargame my heart waged on my brain
or why, miles down the too familiar interstate I pulled over with tears
pin wheeling down my face and tore like a beast
into the greasy breast
wondering why you never kissed me anymore
and at the fact that chickens—
if they wanted to—
could overtake the world;
there are so many more of them than us.

What I Found in the Swamp

It was the bayous that showed us where we'd been,
in that bastard salt freshwater stewing
with alligators and swamp piss. Miles from New
Orleans, I snaked my arm through yours while spray
from the airboat slapped me in the face, not nearly as hard
as your snapping words of the past three years
had managed. Killing
the engine and docking beneath a haggard
cypress tree, roots sprouting and sucking
at air through the marsh, I cradled
a fingerling in frozen hands. Its belly
hung heavy in my palm, trusting stupidly
that I wouldn't crush it for sport, and with only
our thin skins between us, I felt not
even a whisper of heartbeat.

PART SEVEN
LOVE (RESURRECTION)

ASHIATSU IN THE BEDROOM

How much do you weigh? Come,
walk on my back. You treat me like a child,
a Thai prostitute, Buddhist monk,
all the above—and I love it,

the sense of precariousness, one slip and I fall
like a delicate vase, already cracked and chipped
with age and mistakes but for now radiating
pure lightness, my white feet pressing firm and lovely
into the creamed brown hide of your back.
One pound less and I'd vanish,
one pound more and you'd crumble.
My worth is weighed in ounces, your wants
by the ton.

On Beauty and Love

I was the child who found the lumpy pumpkin,
misshapen and abandoned in the fields. At Christmas,
I chose the naked trees, the too short one,
spine a little crooked, needles already browned
and sloughing off like skin. I saw the beauty
in the forgotten ones,
the damaged ones,
the ones with the half off tags,
the living things with their lifelines cut short,
stranded in foreign places—parking lots
and bins outside discount supermarkets.
I wanted to love them, I wanted
them to be loved,
I didn't want to fix them, to hide the bad sides
against the walls
or carve out the bruises with a cheap blade.
This is what beauty is,
and then there was you. You
are my perfect imperfection
and I was the child who found you.

PRODUCE

Some people have penchants
for winning radio contests, others for numbers
of the choice prizes at the bars—the artists or doctors
instead of the waiters or students—but me,
I get the grocery clerks and confused check stand men
at the corner store who give me fruits for free,
tucking them fast as a secret
wrinkled and splitting into paper bags,
but really,
it has nothing to do with luck.
I've always loved the begging for picking fruits.
Not the ones that are just slightly sweeter,
but the bananas with no yellow left to give way to brown,
the plums with skins as finely crinkled
as a grandmother's décolletage, and kiwis
so fragile and soft that even the lightest touch
leaves permanent sloping impressions.
And it's not because I'm cheap,
at least not this time,
it's because I remember the taste of the treasures foraged
from my parent's backyard, the ones beyond the horse pasture
growing from the neighbor's side,
the ones nobody would eat, baking warm in the Oregon sun.
How can something be too sweet?
Like all those people who told us our love was too much,
it must be delayed infatuation, the kind reserved
for teenagers and drunks, like that time you told me
my words were too big to bear their weight and

they'd surely implode one day,
or the time I missed my cycle
and neither of us cried,
not when I called to tell you from California,
or when it crept in shamefully two weeks late
like a dog with his tail slipped between its legs
and we never talked much about it, just sat
side by side shell shocked and amazed at the almost.

'FLORA' AND 'FAWNA'

Gift me peonies and it takes all my strength
to stop myself from beating you senseless, the heavy heads
drunken with blossom, begging for someone to grip them tight
and bludgeon your endless curls with frantic idyllic petals
into an explosion of fragrance. It's the same way
I always ache to trudge through fresh snow, maddened
by the perfection, or to scoop
out that first dollop of peanut butter, the insanity of flawlessness
in the plateau too much to bear, and yet

I've always resisted willpower and a senseless respect
for order, but this,

this weekend in the Gorge, hours on the road trailing
behind us like pollen stains, you pointed a finger thick as God's
to the frozen doe across the median, hooves cemented in time
 steeped into the highway,
her fawn trailing behind, mere leaps
ahead of us.

And when the sedan before us smashed
efflorescence toward the sky, a smattering of horridly stunning
glass, fur, lean limbs—
the body shot beyond the rails—I wanted to soak up that pain,
wrap one of your blueblack curls
around my forefinger,
ask you to bring me peonies in inflorescence
to gush and die,

quietly,

piece by piece, hour by hour, un-missed

and unnoticed in the corner.

KITCHEN VOLCANOES

On the slabs, we pull apart turkey carcasses,
You feed me diced paneer, wet and chilled, in pinched fingers.
It's where you make your evening mess, where I wipe
Up your powders and crumbs, and where the lassi erupts
From our broken blender and bleeds
Into the cracks and pores. Granite is an untamed thing—
Volcanic, unpredictable, a force of a siren.
Deep in the magma chambers, melted rock oozes
And swirls. Sometimes the vile is spewed out in a bulimic fashion
But sometimes,
Sometimes,
It sits in wait for hundreds of thousands of years.
Rocks cool slowly like forgotten indiscretions.
Patience makes the heat forget, the boiling subside. In the end,
Stoicism can erode a mountain, a volcano,
Even you.

Lifetimes later,
Granite rises to the earth's surface, scrubbed clean
And stone cold to strangers, children, everyone but us.
We make countertops from it, slice our dinners,

Spill our drinks and break the glasses.

THE SWEET BELOW THE BITTER

I still want you to make me orange juice, to squeeze,
Press and twist the rinds in your pillowy palms,
To make room
In the freezer because you know that's how I like it,
Enceinte with pulp and buried in a layer of ice
I can crack as easily as your heart. I still listen
To the rhythm every night, the cycle of blood
And all the little things inside you
I'll never know completely—even if I wanted to, even
If I wasn't terrified of the fallout. Let me taste
The carpel, the sweet after the bitter,
And I'll drink it down not caring
Of the trails like slugs left behind.

You're beautiful after the shower, all gingham towels
And weeping curls, your beautiful
Feet melting like spilled butter
Into the hardwood. For me, your beauty
Is the ocean, even the breakers
Can take me down, let alone
The currents—you're undiscovered, you're
Most breathtaking in the unknowing,
The darkness steeped in what I can't see,
Churning in your beauteous tides, inky
With wait,
And pulling at my kicking feet.

PART EIGHT
LOVE (MUMBAI)

Familial Territory

You told me you looked like your father,
your brother like your mother,
but that's not what I saw in the Mumbai tea house.
What everyone told you was wrong,
a lie from their eyes. Your mother
engulfs you both, in the cacao-black
eyes and teeth crowded as a morning train.

Your father, he's slipped into your innards,
entrenched in your turned-down chin,
arms frozen across chest, the cold set
of your jaw, the distance of your aura.
Your father doesn't scare me

because all I see is you. You in thirty years,
the you of our past, over-seasoning tradition
and fear with barricades.
I broke them down once,
I can do it again. They all doubt me

and therein lies my power. It's in my tiny bones,
the reach of my hair, the fray
of my lashes. You know my stubbornness
is thicker than yours, my desire burns brighter
than all the fireworks of Diwali
and your father, the poor man,

will see me one day

just as you do.

Do You See the Stars?

Mumbai. I could live here. No,
I mean I could live here—this
is waking up. Remember
when you pressed your thumbs,
thick and unforgiving,
into my eye sockets, slow as death
until I gave in
to the dizzy and you whispered,
accent sticky, dripping in rose syrup,
Do you see the stars?
And I did. They burst in the darkness like kisses.
This city has a heart, fluttering
crazed and drunken as a beast, fingers
itchy and always wanting, wanting,
a mouth with hunger so palpable
I gave myself in an instant. I was new,
damp when I came here, ridiculous
as one of those puppy mill survivors
too petrified to take a single step from the cage
into green grass and sunshine. I stumbled,
blinded,
but for the stars.
I risked it all for you
because it was home, because it was you,
the cage I left behind, dank and cloying
and so sadly, pathetically familiar. It was a husk,
forgotten like nightmares and used-to-bes,
but it was all I'd ever known.

LURE

The grace and urgency in the chaos hooked me hard,
a hungry and stupid fish
flailing in the sudden lightness of it all,
amidst heavy boots and stomping accents.
I was terrified,
never good at taking tests, and this,
this is what it all came down to.
I smelled nothing of the open sewers,
my heart cracked no more at the grasping
of child beggars, unwilling to explode into confetti
even after all the beatings
you'd given it for five thirsty years.
The heat didn't suffocate or burn,
but wrapped my slight body like a blanket—
for once in my life I was warm.
But it was the secrecy, the touch prohibition
that sparked in me what we'd let go dormant
in the pressing Oregon gray,
the squeeze of a thigh
in the backs of rickshaws,
the kissing of fingertips
when sharing street paan,
the non-accidentals that made me love you
over and over and all over again. And that night,
dosas on banana leaves, daal in silver tins
while I commanded my left hand to stay,
pale and slippery as an Exocoetidae
in my lap while I downed the spiciest dumplings,

the most searing soups,
I swallowed the heat
of 1,826 days until my lower lip split open,
copper slicing fillets down my throat.
You took me to the falooda stand
where the heavy cream licked my wounds
and the mosquitoes tore my legs apart.
I didn't care
about the dengue or malaria or the ugliness
of the unknown, all I knew
was that my body's always betrayed
what my insides hunger after,
and maybe the fish aren't such idiots after all, maybe
they just know what their desires are worth.

SATYAVACHAN

Say something in Gujarati and I see you
As you were years ago, in the bars
Next to gargantuan women, faded flowers
Suckling your youth, moving quick as hummingbirds,
Flashing crow's feet with a deftness
That blurred their age. Feed me by hand
Like you used to, change my water for yours,
The one ringing with ice,
And tell me you love me
Even throughout all the changes
After all these years.

My father told me, Be careful,
You have that wandering way,

Just like him, whom I see in your slowness
To laugh, the oil slicks of your eyes. I chose
You, I choose
An incredible life.

The Things I Do for You

The things I do for you
Are without thinking,
No scores kept or favors stacked.
It's in the simplicity, the ease
That I know now—as I always have—
That loving you is natural, as much
A part of me as my crooked eyebrows.
That's why

I give you the good pieces
Of bread, the thickest morsels
Torn from cookies, the water
With the least ice (I know
How you hate the cold).

My heart is threaded
Into these gestures. Without thought,
Yet over-seasoned with adoration

Are the things I do for you.

SAVING ROOM

A dessert too sweet? That's nonsense
even as a child I never believed.
Give me the corner piece, buttercream
piled high in shells and roses,
Cornelli lace by the foot and sotas for days.

I'd scoop out the cake, an unnecessary social obligation—
like dinner before your mouth on mine,
whiskey before shirts on floors—
and feast on sheer frosting, grains crashing against my teeth
rough as the tide. This

is still how I like it, creamed nipples
and syrup on collarbones, rivering down,
down,
into the devil's food of our bodies,
moist and molten in a way
fondant artists and bakery slaves
never imagined pulling from the heat.

THE PROPOSAL

It wasn't in one of our fancy restaurants,
over plates of raw lamb, deer hearts,
and discs of foie gras melting into woodblock chocolate.
You did it at home,
me in my old pink sweatpants
from the last exotic petting zoo,
you smelling of salt and the hours
buried deep in the lab. It was February,
two weeks after we came back from India,
two weeks after your father's disappointment,
your mother's smile, battered as yours,
two weeks after our nights tucked into street pizza
loaded with sweat and canned cheese.
Every day since we left
you told me one thing about the country
you've spent decades waiting to leave.
In India, if there are many things you want,
you have to bargain. But if there's just one,
one thing you want,
then you have to bribe.

This is how you asked me to marry you.
My hair, greased into a knot, acne
cream on my face, and you
in shining gym clothes, one hand
held a can of sweet cheese that had survived
the aching of 15,720 miles,
in the other a simple loop of gold,

endless.

This is your bribe,

if you let me be your husband.

36 HOURS

The 36 hours after you asked me to marry you,
I didn't sleep.
Instead
I wrote to my friends in the Middle East,
Burrowed down into my work
And practiced balancing the new weight
Of my left hand, wrapped in veins
And slender as spiders' legs. The 36 hours
After you proposed in our kitchen,
The past five years shot memory bullets
Through my body, the fight until dawn
Years ago when I told you
One day you'll tell your parents about me,
One day you'll cry for me
Like you did for your nani, and one day
I'll be gone. The lies
We told each other and ourselves
Got mixed up somehow like a college kid's
Jungle juice, too sweet,
But we,
We were too naïve to know it
and now that the tar of your hair
Has given way to webs of silver
And the wrinkles spooning my eyes
No longer tuck away when I sleep,
You know I was right. In the 36 hours

After we let what was written's ink dry,

Bleeding into the papers and pages of we,
I didn't want to risk a surprise ending,
A slow awakening from a lucid dream,

The kind you get consumed by wholly
On a sun-drowned afternoon and try to dig your way
Out like a crazed animal, nails puncturing mud walls
While you wail like a beast, yet still you slip deeper,
Bloodying your knees and making bargains with God

But to all the rest of the world, you rest
In peace, warmed and comforted by the glow.

RESURRECTION

I never wanted to come back,
Not here, where the mess sloshed over
Like cocktails staining pretty satined feet.
I came back for you, happy
To leave the palm trees behind,
The howler monkeys on the tin roof.
Oregon is where it began, and the Great
Northwest demanded the act end here, too
(That's always where the hook kicks in).
Moving on,
We'll leave the rain behind, the gummy
Bars tired from our twenties, the restaurants plundered
And the rain-pregnant streets already forgetting
Our stampeding feet. I came back
To check for a pulse, see if we
Could be pulled back sharply
From the edge of extinction.
How glorious that our vitality is so strong,
Alive and kicking wildly, strong
Like something shot at close range,
Yet demanding stubbornly to live.

ALL THE UNSAID THINGS

There are times when I'm scared to touch you,
Afraid my fingertips will burst into flame, prints sloughed
Away into ashes,
Unidentifiable,
And the inches between your leg and mine
Are oceans.
When I ask you to tell me all the bad things about me,
You never give me what I want:
That you don't want a baby
Because your goodness isn't strong enough
To cover up all my bad,
That I'm selfish to such a degree
The starvation can't chew up a heart
Already willowed, dried up, and shrunk
Into a prune. There are times
I want to write by hand I am not enough
until I fill a notebook,
My fingers cramping and the words
Becoming a part of me, etched deep
Into my bones.
Is that what it takes to make something mine?
Like the Hindi alphabet or my slanted cursive,
Just tell me all the bad things
And I'll swallow them up like pills,
Like candy so they rest heavy,
Solid and satisfying in my stomach.

THE PROTAGONIST

You got your own book. This
Is our love story, pages
Brimming with remembers:
The close calls, reversed regrets,
Proud colors bleeding out
From the Nehalem days like stiffening pink
Peonies. I can't give you much.

My voice sticks in my teeth like chikki.
But I can give you this—

The best of back whens,
The worst hours wrapped tight for storage
And me

Draped in letters and adorned in poetry.

Author Bio

 Jessica Tyner Mehta is a Pushcart Prize nominee born in Central Point, Oregon and spent much of her adult life in Portland. A graduate of the Ooligan Press program, she received her master's degree in writing from Portland State University, completing the second year of the program interning with The Fulbright Commission in London, England. An extensive traveler, she has lived in England, South Korea, and Costa Rica and has published poetry around the world.

She's the founder of The Jessica Tyner Scholarship Fund, an annual gift for graduate students with a Native American connection who are pursuing an advanced degree in writing or a related field. As a member of the Cherokee Nation, Jessica actively participates in helping to perpetuate the success, artistry, and passion of Native writers.

Li Young-Lee, Maya Angelou, and Pablo Neruda top her list of favorite poets. With confessional leanings, Jessica has long relied on her personal experiences to provide fodder and inspiration for her writing. She believes in the simple idea that words are meant to be read. An entrepreneur, Jessica is the owner of MehtaFor, a business that provides a number of writing services for a variety of industries and clients.

She's also a certified yoga instructor, avid first edition book collector, and has a penchant for old muscle cars and road trips. In her spare time, she enjoys vacationing in Napa Valley, her Trans Am, and spending time with her inspiration for The Last Exotic Petting Zoo, Chintan.

JESSICA TYNER

CPSIA information can be obtained at www.ICGtesting.com
Printed in the USA
BVOW01*1754100914

365975BV00001BA/1/P